W9-ARZ-829

Fish: Keeping & Breeding in Captivity

Guppies

Homer Mozart

Published in association with T.F.H. Publications, Inc.,
the world's largest and most respected publisher of pet literature

Chelsea House Publishers
Philadelphia

CONTENTS

Fish: Keeping & Breeding in Captivity

Aquarium Setting Up
Siamese Fighting Fish
Catfish
Goldfish
Guppies
Marine Aquarium
Piranhas
Tropical Fish
Angelfish

HP BR
J
SF458
.G8
M69
1999x

Publisher's Note: All of the photographs in this book have been coated with FOTOGLAZE™ finish, a special lamination that imparts a new dimension of colorful gloss to the photographs.

Reinforced Library binding & Super-Highest Quality Boards

This edition ©1999 TFH Publications, Inc., 1 TFH Plaza, Neptune City, NJ 07753. This special library bound edition is made expressly for Main Line Book Company a division of Chelsea House Publishers.

Library of Congress Cataloging-in-Publication Data applied for
0-7910-5091-2

Library of Congress Cataloging-in-Publication Data

Mozart, Homer.
  Guppies / Homer Mozart.
    p. cm. — (fish and aquariums)
  Includes index.
  Summary: A guide to keeping guppies, describing the different varieties that exist, breeding strategies, care and feeding, aquarium maintenance, and more.
  ISBN 0-7910-5091-2 (hc)
  1. Guppies--Juvenile literature. 2. Aquariums--Juvenile literature.
  (1. Guppies. 2. Aquariums.) I. Title. II. Series.
  SF458.G8M69 1998
  639.3'7667—dc21
                98-7553
                CIP
                AC

INTRODUCTION

Of the many animal hobby pursuits you could involve yourself in, keeping fishes in an aquarium is undoubtedly one of the most fascinating and relaxing. Compared to other animal hobbies, such as the keeping of mammals or birds, aquarium fishkeeping is a relatively new pursuit, dating back only as far as the 19th Century. It is true that fishes had been kept by humans for many centuries prior to this, but these were maintained in outdoor ponds. Attempts to keep them in relatively small containers were always followed by disaster — the death of the fish in a short span of time.

Not until the chemistry of natural waters was understood could fishkeeping become a hobby. A British surgeon, Ellis, in *The Chemistry of Creation*, published in 1850, was one of the first scientists to document the importance of oxygen and carbon dioxide exchange in the fish/plant symbiosis. A chemist, Robert Warrington, studied the matter in more detail, and it was the English naturalist Philip Henry Gosse who first applied this knowledge in a practical manner.

Gosse built a number of vivariums (the original name applied to what is now an aquarium) and succeeded in maintaining a collection of both freshwater and saltwater fishes for a number of months. His research resulted in the opening of the world's first public

A red snakeskin produced in Singapore by Gan Aquarium Fish Farm.

PHOTO BY CHEW KENG LOON

aquarium at the London Zoo in 1853. Other zoos, in Germany, France and elsewhere, followed suit and featured aquariums. The result was a great upsurge in public demand for information on the keeping of fishes. A new animal hobby was well and truly underway.

However, aquarists in those days were primitive by today's standards. Many millions of fishes died due to insufficient knowledge on the part of the owner—a fact that is still a reality in this hobby at the beginner level. In the early years most attention was directed toward freshwater fishes as home pets, the goldfish quickly establishing itself as the most popular species due to its very hardy and adaptable nature.

The availability of heaters, air pumps, and filters was a major step forward in technology, as it enabled species from warmer waters to be maintained successfully. This gave birth to the tropical fish hobby. It was to be the area of the hobby that would make the most rapid expansion, especially in the years following the end of World War II. Tropical fishes sport a greater array of colors and patterns than those from temperate climates. This alone ensured that they would remain perennial favorites ahead of those generally referred to as "coldwater" fishes, of which the ubiquitous goldfish was and remains the major focus of attention.

THE ARRIVAL OF THE GUPPY

Having given a brief historical backdrop to set the scene, we can now introduce the guppy, the

A blue snakeskin guppy produced by Gan Aquarium Fish Farm in Singapore.

PHOTO BY CHEW KENG LOON.

PHOTO BY CHEW KENG LOON.

The famous Purple Dragon Head Guppy, so named by the Gan Aquarium Fish Farm who produced this fish. The popular names of guppy varieties are usually designated by the breeder who developed the strains. Often the same kind of fish has a different name in each of the international markets.

subject of this book. This tiny fish from South America is named for the English naturalist John Lechmere Guppy, who became incorrectly credited as being its discoverer. He took specimens from Trinidad to England, and the species was named *Girardinus guppyi* in his honor by Günther, the famed zoologist who was head of the British Museum at that time. (The genus *Girardinus* was named by Poey for the naturalist of the Smithsonian Institute, Charles Girard.) However, in 1863, before Guppy made his "discovery," the guppy had been collected and named *Lebistes poeciloides* by the Spaniard De Filippi. (*Lebistes* means "a kind of fish.") To complicate matters even further, the German zoologist J. L. Peters had collected the fish earlier still, in 1859, and named it

Poecilia reticulata (the latter meaning "net-like"). In 1913 the guppy was called *Lebistes reticulatus* by Regan. This was generally accepted until quite recent times, although other names were in use. Today, the name given by Peters back in 1859 takes priority.

Although guppies were imported into Europe and the USA during the latter part of the 19th century, it was not until the 1920s that they started to gain popularity as pets. Indeed, even then there was only limited interest in them. This persisted until about the late 1950s, when concerted efforts there were to selectively breed color variants.

As with any pet, when mutations start to appear there is invariably an explosion of interest in the species. This was very much the case with these tiny fish. During the next two decades they really became fashionable. By the late 1970s there was already an extensive range of colors and fin types, and the development of the guppy has continued to this day. Today, no other fish, including the many gorgeous koi, can rival them in this area. Of all pets, probably only the budgerigar as a single species enjoys a comparable following of dedicated breeders.

THE BASIS OF THE GUPPY'S SUCCESS

Clearly, the multitude of colors, their patterns, and fin shapes, have been the cornerstone on which the guppy's success has been built. But these are by no means the only sources of its appeal; it has many other virtues. The guppy is an excellent community fish, being non-aggressive toward other species. It is arguably the hardiest of all tropical fishes in that it will survive in a range of water temperatures and conditions that few other species, other than perhaps the goldfish, could tolerate. It is a very willing breeder, so much so that if both sexes are present you would find it impossible to stop them from breeding!

Its size is yet another major plus for it as an aquarium fish. You can keep a large number of guppies in a relatively small tank and thus have a magnificent display for a very low financial outlay. It must also be stated that some breeders keep guppies

A wild guppy male.

PHOTO BY MP & C PIEDNOIR, AQUAPRESS.

PHOTO BY CHEW KENG LOON.

1ST PRIZE

GUPPY

VARIEGATED

This tank filled with variegated guppies, all almost identical, won First Prize in the Variegated Guppy Class at the Aquarium Show held in Singapore in 1993.

purely as feeder species for carnivorous fishes. But we are interested only in having them as piscine jewels in their own right.

You really could not begin in this hobby with a better fish, whether you keep them with other species in a community tank, as the focus of your entire display, or as "moving ornaments" for an aquarium that is primarily a display of live plants.

Although guppies are as undemanding a species as you could find, nonetheless they cannot be abused if they are to be healthy and impressive aquarium occupants. Likewise, if breeding is to be undertaken, it is important that you take this very seriously; otherwise, you will soon become disenchanted in the steady deterioration that will ensue if carefully planned breeding is not the order of the day. In the following chapters is all the basic information you need to know.

WHAT IS A GUPPY?

You do not need to have the knowledge of an ichthyologist in order to maintain and breed guppies successfully. But a basic understanding of what a guppy is all about will be useful. If you are a first-time aquarist you should also understand a little about the ways fishes are broadly grouped in hobby circles.

WHERE FISHES LIVE

Over 70% of the earth's surface is covered by water, most of it by large seas and oceans that are rich in salts. This latter fact has a considerable bearing on the types of water fishes have evolved to live in. This provides our first major division of fishes from a hobby viewpoint: marine and freshwater. The guppy is one of the latter.

Marine fishes live in an environment that has a greater

Freshwater fishes have the reverse problem. Their body fluids are denser than the water they live in, and water constantly diffuses into their bodies. Thus, they drink little, if at all, while releasing large amounts of urine. In actual fact, the guppy, like the goldfish, is capable of living in

PHOTO BY CHEW KENG LOON.

The fabled Green Diamond Guppy developed by Gan Aquarium Fish Farm in Singapore.

density than the fluids in the fish's body. Via a process known as *osmosis*, marine fishes are constantly losing water to the surrounding environment, so must drink copious amounts of it in order to remain at equilibrium. These fishes also release minimal fecal matter, and that which is excreted is high in salts. Excess salts that marine fishes gain when they drink seawater is actively pumped out through cells in the gill filaments.

mildly saline waters that would kill many freshwater fishes. But for all practical purposes you should regard this species as a freshwater fish.

You may astutely be aware that eels, salmon, and sticklebacks, to name but three species, move from one type of water to the other during certain periods of their lives. (These fishes are called *diadromous*.) They have very specialized kidneys and other physiological modifications that enable them to do this.

The inability of most freshwater fishes to survive in salt water has an important side effect when it comes to eradicating parasites and other pathogens. This is worthy of mention. Most parasites also have evolved to live in either fresh or salt water, but not both. If they are subjected to waters not conducive to their metabolism, it always near freezing, while in the tropics it usually is warm. (However, the depth of the water, the elevation, and the speed at which it is flowing also will affect temperature.) Temperature gives us the second major division within the aquatic hobby, tropical vs. temperate, but this parameter is much more flexible than is

The blue variegated snakeskin guppy produced by Gan Aquarium Fish Farm.

will effect their ability to regulate their water content. Their body cells will either swell excessively and literally burst, or implode due to excessive loss of fluid. This is why short-term saltwater baths are very effective in the treatment of some parasite problems in freshwater fishes.

THE TEMPERATURE FACTOR

There is a considerable range in the temperature of waters found on Earth. In polar regions it is

tolerance to salinity.

There are coldwater species, such as the goldfish, and tropical fishes, the guppy being one of the latter. However, the guppy has the ability to survive in cooler waters that would certainly kill most tropical fishes. It is this ability to withstand a wide range of conditions, which includes water hardness and pH values, that makes the guppy one of the most adaptable of fishes.

This does not mean that

guppies should be subjected to sudden changes or steady abuse of their water conditions. It means that as a species they have the ability to adapt to a range of conditions if these are introduced slowly and thereafter remain constant.

It should also be noted that inbred strains, especially those that show considerable divergence in form and color from the wild type, are far less able to withstand change. The reason that this is so lies in the fact that the mutations that create these beautiful strains and individuals may bring with them minor physiological changes. These affect membrane permeability and gill function, as well as other aspects of metabolism. Taken together, they make the individual less able to adapt than the wild types, and thus more vulnerable to changes in their watery world.

METHODS OF REPRODUCTION

Apart from dividing fishes into groups based on the salinity of the water and its temperature, hobbyists also distinguish between the way fishes reproduce. Those fishes (the majority) that lay eggs that hatch outside of the female's body are called egglayers, the technical term being *oviparous*. This is a rather wasteful method of reproduction because most of the eggs will quickly be eaten or perish in other ways.

Some evolutionarily recent fishes developed ways to reduce the number of eggs needed and ensuring that a greater percentage of young would survive. Although other strategies are used by fishes, livebearing is a

This purple guppy was a true strain perfected and marketed by Gan Aquarium Fish Farm in Singapore.

PHOTO BY CHEW KENG LOON.

PHOTO BY CHEW KENG LOON.

This magnificent green guppy with a solid yellow tail was given the strain name Yellowtail by Gan Aquarium Fish Farm, the producer of this fish.

major one. Livebearing species, of which the guppy is one, retain the eggs in the female's body until they have hatched. They live off the small yolks of the eggs but also get some nourishment directly from the mother. The fry are born as diminutive replicas of their parents. Only about 500 or so of the 20,000-plus fish species are included within this group, but they are among the most popular of aquarium fishes. Livebearers also include the mollies, platies, swordtails, goodeids, and a few odds and ends.

Livebearers are of two types. In one, the eggs are merely retained within the ovaries or oviduct and develop mainly from nutrients derived from the yolk included in their yolk sac. These are called *ovoviviparous*. In the other type, the embryos are nourished by the female via placenta-like structures; these are the "true" livebearers, or *viviparous* fishes. The guppy is usually said to be ovoviviparous; however, as we noted, there definitely is some maternal contribution to the nourishment of the embryos, so you will appreciate that the distinction between the two methods is not a clear-cut line.

In order to deposit sperm into the female, the livebearers had to develop a sort of penis. This was achieved by modifying part of the anal fin into a copulatory organ known as a *gonopodium*. When breeding, the gonopodium of the guppy is rotated forward and usually to one side. It forms a tube for the passage of packets of sperm (*spermatophores*) into the oviduct of the female so that they can fertilize the ripe eggs in the ovaries.

PHOTO BY CHEW KENG LOON.

A golden snakeskin guppy produced by Gan Aquarium Fish Farm. Gan exports to markets all over the world and might well be the world's largest producer of both guppies and discus.

Female guppies have the ability to store some of these "packets" in the ovaries so that they can be used to fertilize eggs at a latter date. This adaptation is seen in all poeciliids. If you were not aware of this ability you would be surprised if you obtained some female guppies and noted that they produced offspring in the absence of a male. Guppies are not hermaphroditic (both sex organs in the same individual), or parthenogenetic (capable of reproduction without the need for a male to fertilize the eggs).

THE GUPPY: A DESCRIPTION

With a basic understanding of where the guppy fits into the aquarium hobby, we can now focus more closely on it as an individual species.

Distribution: The original distribution of the guppy is northeastern South America (Brazil to Venezuela) and the islands of Trinidad, Barbados, and others nearby. It has been introduced into many countries, both tropical and temperate, in order to help eradicate mosquito larvae. Thus, its distribution in the tropics is now pretty much cosmopolitan.

Habitat: The guppy is found in shallow rivers, streams, lakes, lagoons, and estuaries where the water may be fresh or brackish.

Size: The female is larger, reaching 2.4 inches (6 cm); the male grows to 1.4 inches (3.5 cm).

Color: The basic wild-type color pattern is very variable, but comprises silver, green, brown, blue, red, and black. The females are much more somber in coloration than the males, though through selective breeding they have become more appealing. By the same process, the very ordinary-looking male wild guppy has become a piscine jewel that can sport a whole rainbow of colors.

Fins: The guppy sports typical fish finnage in that it has single dorsal, caudal (tail), and anal fins, plus paired pectoral and pelvic (ventral) fins. The dorsal is short and begins just behind the midline of the body. The paired pelvics are situated well behind the pectorals, but anterior to the dorsal, and just forward of the anal. The latter has been modified in the male to form the gonopodium already discussed.

The dorsal and caudal fins display tremendous variation in domestic guppies, where, through selective breeding of mutations, they have become both larger and quite variable in shape.

Mouth: The mouth is terminal and superior. This latter term means its opens dorsally and indicates that the guppy generally is a surface feeder, which of course is where it would snatch mosquito larvae, small insects, and similar prey. The mouth features membranous lips that are well supplied with sensory nerve endings.

Other Anatomical Features: The guppy is a very typical fish in that its body is covered with scales, it has a two-chambered heart, kidneys, and other organs found in all vertebrate animals. One organ, the gas or swim bladder, is

The green snakeskin guppy bred by Gan Aquarium Fish Farm in Singapore.

PHOTO BY CHEW KENG LOON.

Not every strain is a winner. This Ocelot Guppy developed by Gan wasn't a financial success.

This magnificent variegated lower swordtail guppy was produced and photographed by Tanaka in Japan.

worthy of comment. This organ is useful to many fishes because it acts as a hydrostatic mechanism that enables the fish to move between different water depths, or to remain motionless at a given depth without expending undue amounts of energy. Fish flesh is denser than water, so the fish achieves neutral buoyancy by adjusting the amount of gases in the bladder, thus changing the overall density of its body. As the gases are reduced the density increases and the fish will start to sink; as the bladder is filled the density drops and the fish will rise. The fish increases or reduces the gaseous content of its swim bladder by the secretion or absorption of gases directly from or to the blood.

If you would like to learn more about the anatomy and physiology of fishes, your pet shop should have some good general books on ichthyology.

PHOTO COURTESY OF GAN AQUARIUM FISH SARM

The Blue Diamond Guppy produced by Gan is a best seller.

UNDERSTANDING WATER QUALITY

You undoubtedly are aware that water can have many tastes or flavors depending on its source. In part, such tastes are created by the minerals and chemicals from the natural environment, as well as those that may or may not have been added to it to make it safe to drink. The amounts of gases (oxygen, carbon dioxide, ammonia, etc.) also are important. If water flows over rocks that are rich in calcium and other soft minerals it will be hard and usually alkaline. If it flows over land that contains much organic material it will be acidic and usually soft.

The temperature of a body of water (such as that in your aquarium) will have an influence over the amount of oxygen it can contain. The warmer it is, the less dissolved oxygen it can hold. This, in turn, affects the number of fishes that can be accommodated. However, more important is the surface area of the water, because it is at this interface that oxygen enters the water and carbon dioxide and other gases leave. The greater the surface area, the greater the amount of oxygen that can be dissolved. The smaller the area, the less oxygen that can be held, almost regardless of depth.

The cleanliness of the water is a significant factor in fishkeeping success. Uneaten food, the decaying leaves of plants, fecal matter from fishes, and other organic matter will all tend to produce levels of ammonia, nitrites, phosphates and other compounds that can be lethal to your fishes, i.e., beyond their levels of tolerance. They will not only affect the oxygen and carbon dioxide content of the water, but they will also negatively affect the mucus layer that protects the fish's skin. Once this is impaired, parasites and other pathogens (disease-causing organisms) may attack the fish. Very soon it will be unhealthy and make the water even more dangerous for other fishes by exposing them to high levels of pathogens.

Natural waters retain their ecological stability—be this very fresh and clean, somewhat dirty, brackish, hard, acidic, and so on— by the forces of nature they are subject to. Winds, rain, the ever-moving nature of water, its considerable volume, the migratory nature of some fishes (even if over a small distance) and the plants and other organisms (large predators to microscopic animals) in the water, all help to create a natural balance to which all its life forms have adapted.

But in the aquarium these forces are not present. Unless you continually compensate for them with sound husbandry, the water quality will rapidly degenerate. Controlling water quality at a level that is acceptable to all the inhabitants of a system is a big part of what the hobby is all about.

This does not mean you must be forever checking the pH or other values, for over-attention can sometimes be as detrimental as a lack of it. A common-sense approach that combines a keen sense of observation of conditions, and of the fish, is more important than meddling with conditions when this would be inappropriate. Consistency of routine is what you should aim for. With the help of mechanical aids (filters, etc.) it is now possible to maintain virtually any type of water so that it remains clean and largely free from contaminants and unwanted organisms.

What you must remember is that when you first set up an aquarium the water is by no means "mature" enough to maintain a collection of guppies. It must be carefully prepared so that vital biological processes can begin. You also must monitor pH, hardness, and temperature, to be sure they are suited to the species, in this case guppies, that are to live in that water.

The wise aquarist will therefore prepare the aquarium at least two or more weeks before the fish are introduced. When the water quality appears to be stabilized at the required levels, only then should a few guppies be introduced. The aquarium still requires more weeks to further mature after the initial fish are added. Thereafter, additional stock can only be accommodated on a gradual basis.

An aquarium may be compared to a fine wine. You cannot rush its maturation, in spite of the additives that can help these days, you must allow this to happen on a gradual basis for the very best results.

pH

The pH of water is a measure of its acidity or alkalinity. A scale of 0-14 is used, where 7.0 is the neutral point. Below this is acidic, the more so as you approach 0. Above 7.0 is alkaline. A movement of 1.0 up or down the scale represents a tenfold increase in acidity or alkalinity; for example, water with a pH of 6.0 is ten times more acidic than water of 7.0.

PHOTO COURTESY OF AQUARIUM PHARMACEUTICALS.

Every aquarist must have the ability to test the quality of the aquarium water. Water test kits are available at most pet shops.

The guppy is best kept within the range of pH 6.8-7.4. Fortunately, this is a range into which domestic tap water frequently falls. The pH will fluctuate depending on temperature, type of gravel used, oxygen content, uneaten foods, and other organic debris created. It is best to test the water at the same time of day when monitoring regularly, so that 24-hour fluctuations do not give you what might appear to be incorrect readings.

Test kits are stocked by your pet shop and come complete with all instructions. There are various types which use either a liquid reagent, powder, or tablets. There are also several models of electronic pH monitors, but these are expensive, though very accurate and easy to use. Make sure that any test kit or monitor you obtain will measure in the 6.0-7.6 range, which encompasses our target range for guppies.

AMMONIA (NH_3)

This is a gas that is very soluble in water and is produced by fishes as a waste product, as well as by the bacterial breakdown of organic matter in the aquarium.

Beyond 0.2 mg per liter (possibly even a little lower) it may be lethal to your fish. Eventually, beneficial bacteria will grow in your filter and gravel that will convert the ammonia to nitrite (NO_2). Nitrite is still dangerous, but a little less so than ammonia—0.5 mg/liter is the lethal point. The good news is that other bacteria convert the nitrite to nitrate (NO_3), which is relatively safe up to 100 mg/liter. These chemical processes are called the *nitrogen cycle* (because all the compounds contain nitrogen), and the bacterial processes that convert ammonia to nitrite to nitrate are the basis of *biological filtration.*

Ammonia toxicity is linked to pH: in water that has a pH below 7.0, the effects of ammonia are reduced, while in alkaline water they are sharply amplified. Test kits are available for ammonia, nitrite, and nitrate, but the interrelationship of these chemicals in the nitrogen cycle is such that for all practical purposes only one is needed. That for nitrites is suggested. If nitrites are low, it means the nitrogen cycle is functional and ammonia is being converted to nitrite and then to nitrate.

It is worth mentioning that many beginners mistake nitrite poisoning for oxygen starvation in newly set-up tanks simply because they see the fishes gasping at the surface. This is a common reaction of fishes to many different toxins because toxins damage gill tissues, so the fishes try to breathe the oxygen-rich air right at the surface. This is why it is so important to test for nitrite.

WATER HARDNESS

The amount of salts in the water makes the water hard or soft. When you boil a kettle of hard water, you are no doubt aware of the lime that forms. The same is true of lime that builds up in domestic water heaters and pipes. Fishes have evolved to live in waters within given hard or soft water ranges. If these are not supplied their gills, fins, and internal organs will be negatively effected, and breeding results will suffer badly as well.

Hardness is measured in numerous ways, but the two most popular methods are parts per million (ppm) of calcium carbonate ($CaCO_3$), or degrees of hardness (dH), which indicate the parts of calcium oxide (CaO) per 100,000 parts of water.

Understanding the chemistry of hardness is complex, but using one of the available test kits makes things simple for you.

The guppy is best suited to hardness in the range of dH 10-30°, which is equal to 180-540 ppm. This translates to water that is medium to hard, with a dH of 12-18° possibly being the preferred state.

CHLORINE & CHLORAMINE

Chlorine is a gas that readily dissolves in water, and which has a destructive effect on the respiratory tract. It is easily dissipated into the atmosphere if water is allowed to stand for 24 hours, or if it is vigorously stirred. Chloramines are compounds of chlorine and ammonia that are much more stable than chlorine gas, so are not as easily removed from water. Both are added to domestic water supplies in order to kill pathogens, so must be removed before fishes are introduced. Test kits are produced for chlorine and chloramine. Your pet shop will

The Blond Diamond Guppy produced in Singapore by Gan Aquarium Fish Farm.

PHOTO BY CHEW KENG LOON.

A wonderful blue variegated guppy with a black body. The fish was produced at Gan Aquarium Fish Farm in Singapore.

also have chemicals designed to neutralize chlorine and chloramines.

OTHER CHEMICALS IN THE WATER

Although the number of other chemicals in water is many, one or two should be mentioned. Copper is a potentially lethal element for fishes beyond certain tolerances. For this reason, it is always wise to run a faucet for 30 seconds before using the water. This removes copper or metals that may be in your tap water from your pipes.

Phosphate is another chemical compound that should be tested for if the water is suffering from algal bloom (an excess of algal growth that turns the water green).

You also can obtain dissolved oxygen and carbon dioxide test kits, but these normally are unnecessary for the guppy hobbyist.

ADJUSTING WATER PROPERTIES

There are numerous ways in which you can adjust the properties of the water until it is satisfactory for your needs. Your pet shop sells a wide range of water conditioners for different purposes, such as removing chlorine, copper, and other gases, metals or compounds. Filtration will also help in this direction, as discussed in the next chapter.

Hardness and pH can be adjusted by adding or removing

calcareous rocks and gravel, and by the addition of specific resins, or aquarium peat. The addition of acids directly to established tanks to lower pH is not advised and should be done (if at all) in water prepared before it is added to the tank. You can also reduce alkalinity and hardness by dilution with rain or distilled water until the required levels are established.

DOMESTIC WATER

The water you obtain from your tap is the most convenient way in which to supply your aquarium. However, because it is treated with so many chemicals it cannot be used as is: it must be prepared before using it for the fishes. Furthermore, do not assume that any readings you have obtained from your domestic supply are valid months, or even weeks, later. Following heavy rains or flooding, water authorities will increase the amount of this or that chemical to reinforce hygiene. This can cause havoc for the less-than-diligent aquarists who assume that their tap water is of a constant quality.

WATER CHANGES

As we noted earlier, buildups of wastes and other organic matter occur in the aquarium. In order to avoid the risk of chemical saturation to a potentially lethal level, it is wise to make regular partial water changes. In addition to diluting wastes and other chemicals, water changes may reduce some of the pathogens that are ever-present in any tank. It also

A magnificent golden snakeskin guppy produced by Gan Aquarium Fish Farm.

PHOTO BY CHEW KENG LOON.

has a tonic effect on the fish. Hobbyists differ considerably as to how often and how much water should be changed. A general guide would be about 20% every two weeks (taken from the lower levels, where the most pollutants will be), but the size of the aquarium, the number of fish and plants, as well as the extent of detritus that is observed, will all influence this decision. With guppies, it is safe to say that you should change as much water as you can, as often as you can.

When making water changes you must of course ensure that the new water is of the correct temperature.

PHOTO BY CHEW KENG LOON.

Gan took first prize in the variegated guppy classification at an Aquarama Guppy Show held in Singapore.

Regular partial water changes are a necessity for your guppies' health. These changes can be made without siphons and buckets by using a labor saving automatic water changer.

PHOTO COURTESY OF AQUARIUM PRODUCTS.

A difference of one or two degrees will not harm the fish, but larger fluctuations could induce stress and shock, which obviously are undesirable. Likewise, you must ensure that there are no sudden changes to the pH and hardness. Always remember that most fishes can adjust to slow changes in their environment, but those that are abrupt will be deleterious to their health.

When first reading about water quality and some of the equipment for measuring and treating it, you may think that the hobby will be difficult for you. This will not be so—things will quickly fall into place. What is important is that you do not rush into stocking a new tank and by so doing place the lives of the fish at risk simply because water conditions were not carefully prepared.

By taking your time in ensuring that the water has matured, you not only gain practical knowledge, but can make mistakes without having them prove too costly.

THE TANK AND ITS EQUIPMENT

The first thing you should be aware of is that bigger is most definitely better when it comes to selecting an aquarium. Furthermore, a simple, old-fashioned rectangular tank is superior to fancy designs that are tall, round, or in other ways fashioned with esthetics rather than practicality in mind.

The advantages that large tank sizes provide are numerous: 1) They retain stable water quality more readily. As a result, routine maintenance is reduced. 2) They retain their temperature better. In the event of a short-duration power loss they will not lose heat as quickly as smaller tanks. On a water-volume to heat-cost basis they are more economic than smaller units. 3) Their extra space provides for more interesting aquascaping, and for concealing in-tank equipment such as filters and air lines. 4) They will accommodate more fish. 5) They are more impressive from an esthetic standpoint.

The foregoing comments are applicable to a typical home display tank. Breeders will use smaller units for breeding their guppies, as well as for hospitalization and quarantine purposes. You will appreciate that the more costly units will generally have a longer service life, and probably will be made using superior glass. As a general guide, a tank of 15-30 gallons will do nicely for most needs of the casual guppy hobbyist. If you prefer (and can afford) a more impressive unit, a larger tank can be selected. However, do bear in mind that water is very heavy, so you should make sure that the spot you've chosen can support the weight of the filled tank.

The following information will enable you to calculate volume and weight data for any tank.

Volume = Length x Width x Height

3,785 cubic cm = 1 US gallon

231 cubic in = 1 US gallon

1 Imperial (UK) gallon = 1.2 US gallons = 4.55 Liters

1 US Gallon = 0.833 UK gallons = 3.785 Liters

1 US gallon weighs 8.345lb (3.8kg)

1 UK gallon weighs 10lb (4.55kg)

1 Liter weighs 1kg or 2.2lb

1 Liter = 61cu.in or 1,000 cu. cm

Surface area = Length x width

When selecting your aquarium, do purchase one that comes complete with a full hood with lights. This reduces heat loss and water loss through evaporation.

STOCKING LEVELS

There are many factors that will determine the potential maximum stocking level of an aquarium. Among these are: 1) The water temperature. The cooler it is, the more oxygen it can contain. 2) Its

PHOTO BY AQUA PRESS, MC & P. PIEDNOIR.

Singapore and Japan produce lovely guppies, but Europe and the USA produce magnificent guppies as well. This is a tank filled with golden snakeskins. They all look very much alike and this is the objective of most guppy breeding programs.

cleanliness. Dirty water will hold less oxygen than clean water. 3) The bulk of the fish (its girth). The greater this is, the greater the fish's oxygen consumption. 4) The activity level of the fish. The more active it is, the more oxygen it requires. (Temperature also will influence activity level). 5) The extent of plantings. Live plants consume oxygen during night hours, though it is not a major factor. 6) The chemical composition of the water. This will affect both the amount of oxygen that can be held, as well as the activity and respiratory rate of the fish. 7) The surface area of the water. Oxygen is dissolved into water at the water/atmosphere interface. For practical purposes, the depth of the water is of little consequence. It provides for more space for the fish and plants, and will affect the amount of light that

will reach the lower levels. In very tall tanks it will produce temperature stratification in the absence of ancillary equipment to create circulation.

Clearly, the complexity of these various factors could make stocking level calculations a nightmare. Fortunately, aquarists have established a rule of thumb that works well enough to be a useful guide. It is that a typical tank that is maintained correctly, and without the need for additional equipment, can be stocked at the rate of one inch (2.5cm) of fish (not including the tail) per gallon of water, or one inch of fish or for every 12 square inches (78 square cm) of surface area.

As an example, a tank 24 x 12 x 12in (60 x 30 x 30cm) has a surface area of 288 square inches (1890 square cm). This means it

Green double swordtail guppy produced by Gan Aquarium Fish Farm.

PHOTO BY CHEW KENG LOON.

PHOTO BY CHEW KENG LOON.

Gan's interpretation of a ribbon tail guppy.

can accommodate 24 in (60cm) of fish. If the average guppy length (male-female mix) is 1.5 in (3.8 cm), the stocking level is 16 fish. You must bear in mind that if you base the number on juveniles you will be able to stock more fish—but as they mature you will have overstocked the aquarium.

The stocking level quoted may not seem very high and is worthy of further comment. It assumes a tank is not fitted with auxiliary equipment, and is a natural biological entity (which can never really be the case) in which only partial water changes are made. In reality, stocking levels can be considerably increased if we can increase the oxygen content of the water, and remove the higher quantities of fecal matter and other toxins.

This can be achieved with aeration and filtration equipment. What must be considered is that if these should fail to operate for any reason (breakdown or power loss), conditions in the tank will rapidly deteriorate, the more so the smaller the aquarium, and major problems will quickly result.

The wise aquarist will therefore never risk excessive stocking of a tank simply because the equipment makes this possible. A balanced judgment is the answer, in which a few extra fish are included, but not so many as might create stress, bullying, and pushing the filter system to overload potential.

AERATION

The object of aeration is to disturb the water surface by passing air through one or more diffuser stones attached to a tube connected to a small air pump. The result is a stream of bubbles that rise and burst at the surface.

It is the effect of this bursting that creates miniature waves, and these effectively increase the surface area of the water so it can take up more oxygen.

This stated, we can now consider a basic misconception about these bubbles. Little if any oxygen is absorbed into the water from the bubbles themselves. It is their effect on the surface area that is the all-important factor. As the bubbles rise they also have a secondary effect. They draw water up behind them in the partial vacuum they create. Thus, they help to take unwanted gases to the surface, and help in creating circulation of the water, which is further aided by the use of one or more heaters.

The bubble size is of some importance. If it is too large it rises too quickly to draw water behind it all they way to the top, if it is too small, it does not hold sufficient air to disturb the surface enough to provide maximum aeration, nor does it provide maximum circulation. Some experimentation is always needed to obtain a satisfactory balance.

Simple aeration can almost double the stocking capacity of an aquarium. It can also be used to create esthetic appeal. Ceramic diffuser stones are the preferred choice. These can be small or large in order to create single or multiple columns of bubbles. They can be discretely hidden at the back of the tank, or placed into an ornament.

There are two types of pumps you can choose from. One is the diaphragm type; the other works by piston action. The former is the cheaper and most popular. It should be sited above the tank (to remove the risk of back-siphoning in the event of a power outage) either suspended or placed on a non-slip surface; otherwise, it will tend to "skate" around and cause noise. Pumps come in a number of sizes, depending on how much air is provided. The airflow can be controlled by a knob on some models, or by clamps or valves on the connected air line(s).

FILTRATION

If an efficient filter system is part of your setup, it removes the need for a separate aerator because it can perform this function itself. The filter can be of the foam, canister, box, undergravel, or wheel type, the lattermost being the latest concept. So, there are lots of choices, each offering its own advantages in efficiency, size, or cost.

Rather than discuss the merits of various filter types, it is better that you understand how filtration is achieved. You can then discuss your particular needs with your pet shop personnel. The objects of filtration are: 1) To remove large unwanted materials in suspension, such as uneaten food, fecal matter, and the like. 2) To remove dangerous gases, such as ammonia. 3) To remove dangerous compounds, such as nitrites, or to create an environment in which beneficial bacteria will convert them to nitrates that can be used as a food by plants. 4) To remove various unidentified compounds that may either "color" the water, or that may be harmful to the fish. 5) To remove any residual medicines that may from time to time be used in the aquarium.

Removal is achieved in one of three ways: 1) Mechanical: The

In reality, the three methods may overlap. For example, a mechanical filter using foam or gravel will provide a surface for beneficial bacteria to live on, as will zeolite, which is essentially a chemical filter. Live plants act in all three capacities, while the aquarium substrate provides mechanical and biological filtration.

PHOTO BY CHEW KENG LOON.

A Gan tuxedo Guppy.

water is passed through a material, such as foam or polyester floss, that effectively blocks the passage of solids. 2) Chemical: The water is passed through a medium, such as charcoal or zeolite, which absorbs gases and other chemicals. 3) Biological: The water is passed over a medium rich in beneficial bacteria that convert ammonia and nitrites into the less dangerous nitrates, which are utilized by plants as fertilizer.

However, biological filtration can only be achieved if the water surrounding the medium is rich in oxygen, because the bacteria are *aerobic*, meaning they utilize oxygen for their chemical processing.

Whatever filtration system is used, the water can be returned to the surface so that it agitates this, thus aerating it. It can be returned via a spray bar, which increases the aeration because the water is exposed to the atmosphere as it falls onto the surface.

However, guppies are native to relatively slow-moving waters, so excessive water movement is not essential. Filters should be so arranged that they draw the water from just above the substrate, where it will be the dirtiest and least-aerated.

It is essential that whatever system is used it must be maintained on a regular basis, otherwise the filter will become clogged and ineffective, indeed dangerous. Partial water changes are still needed regardless of how good the filter system is.

HEATING

Guppies prefer a temperature in the range of 72-78°F (22-26°C), though they can cope with variables above or below this. The important thing about heat is that it should be constant, not fluctuating, which rapidly induces stress and chills, thus leading to more serious ailments.

A rule-of-thumb guide to the heater capacity is 5 watts per gallon. A 15-gallon tank will therefore need a 75-watt heater. This assumes a typical home environment. If the tank is large, say, 40 gallons or larger, the watts per gallon can be reduced to about 3.5, because the larger water volume is able to retain its heat much better than a smaller volume.

In very large tanks it is wise to use two heaters whose combined wattage is as desired, or a little above this. It avoids the possibility that if a heater fails the temperature will fall dramatically; you always have a backup. Do not

A blond tuxedo guppy developed by Gan Aquarium Fish Farm.

PHOTO BY CHEW KENG LOON.

Two male Gan Tuxedo's developed at the Gan Aquarium Fish Farm in Singapore.

use a heater that is too powerful for the volume of water to be heated. If the thermostat should stick in the "on" position the heater may take the temperature way above normal, and before you notice the problem it may "cook" the fish!

Heaters are available in a range of types, but the most popular are the combined heater/thermostat submersibles that feature a temperature dial and a pilot light. As a back-up indicator that the water temperature is as required, you should have a thermometer placed at the opposite end of the aquarium from the heater. This should be checked daily as a matter of routine. Your pet shop stocks a range of models. It is prudent to always keep a spare heater on hand.

LIGHTING

Light is required for your aquarium to achieve two major biological functions, plus those that are esthetic. It is vital for plant growth and for the general well-being of the fish, whose feeding and swimming activities are determined by light/dark cycles. If overhead artificial light is not included the fish may start to swim at an angle, and plants may grow toward the direction of whatever light there is (usually daylight entering the front of the tank). The type and intensity of artificial light used will greatly influence the appearance of colors.

The desired light/dark cycle is 12 hours, which approximates the cycle found in tropical regions. With regard to the wattage required, general guide lines are as follows (using fluorescent lighting):

Tank Length Method: 10 watts for every 12 in (30cm) of length.

Surface Area Method: 10 watts for every 140 square inches (900 square cm).

Volume Method: 1.5 watts per gallon if the tank is of rectangular size and a depth comparable with the width.

With regard to the type of lighting needed, you will need to experiment a little to find the one that best suits your plants. There are those that have a bias towards the red or blue end of the spectrum, and are best for plants. These will also enhance certain of the guppy's colors, while creating a rather false impression of others. Conversely, natural daylight tubes, which highlight the natural color of your fish, are not quite as good for plant growth. In a larger tank you use one of each, but for smaller ones you may have to choose one or the other.

There are very many variables that can affect both heat and light requirements. These are subjects you should delve further into. There are many good books available at your local pet shop.

A lovely variegatd blue snakeskin guppy developed by Gan Aquarium Fish Farm.

PHOTO BY CHEW KENG LOON.

SETTING UP A DISPLAY TANK

Before you begin setting up your display tank, again, consider its site with care. Avoid placing it where it may be subjected to drafts—such as opposite doors. Likewise, it should not be so placed that it will receive long hours of direct sunlight. Apart from the risk of overheating, the rays of the sun may encourage strong algal growth at the front and sides of the tank.

THE SUBSTRATE

To provide both a pleasing look and a good surface for beneficial bacteria to live on, a substrate of gravel is required. This should be neither too large nor too small. The latter packs tightly and does not allow for large bacterial colonization or for plant roots, while the former provides too many spaces for uneaten food and debris to collect. A particle size in the range of 2-3 mm is about right.

Avoid using any material containing calcium and magnesium carbonates, as these will make the water too alkaline. Examples are chalk, dolomite, marble, and coral. The best gravel and rocks are granite, slate, sandstone, and similar hard rocks that are chemically neutral in water, thus not affecting its composition. You should obtain your gravel and rocks from pet shops only, but even these should be routinely washed a number of times before being used. This will remove any dust and debris that would otherwise cloud the water. Careful cleaning of everything placed into your aquarium should become your normal routine. It really does reduce the risk of introducing toxins or pathogens into the water.

DECORATIONS

Among the many items that can be used for decorating your display are bogwood and driftwood, roots, cork (weighted), bamboo, and any of the many excellent synthetic rocks, wood, and plants now produced for aquarists. All of these will take on a more natural look as they become covered with algae, on which the fish will browse. Avoid jagged rocks.

Aquarists fall into two broad types. There are those who try to create a very natural look to their aquascape, even though it may not be a faithful reproduction of the habitat of the fishes they keep. There are also those who enjoy novelty effects using colored gravel, sunken ships, and ruins of bygone civilizations. Beauty is in the eye of the beholder, so whatever maintains your interest in the hobby is quite acceptable.

PLANTS

A number of roles are played by plants in an aquarium. Foremost to most aquarists is their beauty—the range of greens, reds, and blue-browns they can

PHOTO COURTESY OF BLUE RIBBON PET PRODUCTS.

Decorative items to be used in an aquarium should be designed specifically for use in an aquarium. Many products are toxic and poison the tank by slowly releasing toxins into the water. Only use ornaments you buy at your local aquarium shop.

produce is matched only by the considerable variety of their leaf shapes and growth habits. But they serve an important biological function in helping to keep the water healthy. They remove nitrates, various salts, and a number of other elements and compounds from the water.

They provide sheltered spots for the fish to rest in, as well as refuge for small fry, or from other fishes if these are kept in a community tank alongside the peaceful guppies. Finally, they are a source of food for the guppies, who will browse on the algae they attract, as well as on the microorganisms that live on them.

Of course, you can purchase many synthetic plants that will serve most of these functions, although they will not be chemical and biological filters. Many hobbyists combine living plants with artificial plants, and to very good effect. What you must always appreciate is that plants are as demanding as the fish are of appropriate water conditions. They have evolved to live in certain waters—acidic, alkaline, hard or soft, and at preferred temperatures, just like your guppies. Indeed, many plants will be more demanding of water conditions than will the fish. Some are very hardy, others extremely delicate. Some like bright lighting; others softer, more diffused light. Each of these needs must be taken into account before they are purchased.

When choosing plants it is best to select only a few and make a good display of these rather than to try to establish a botanical garden of species in your aquarium. Select shorter plants for the foreground, larger ones for the sides and rear of the aquarium. Avoid making things too formal and symmetrical. Large rocks and driftwood placed off-center are much more pleasing on the eye than if they occupy center stage.

You will probably find that certain plants regarded as difficult or easy to establish by some aquarists may not be so in your aquarium. This comment holds true for fishes and many other animals as well, meaning that you must experiment to find the ones that thrive for you and the conditions you have created in your mini-ecosystem.

Your pet shop can advise you as to which plants are best suited to your needs. At the same time, you are advised to research more on plants with respect to their requirements and methods of propagation.

USEFUL TOOLS

The final things you will need before you are ready to set up your display do not cost much, but will be needed time and again. These include a length of plastic piping for siphoning purposes, one or two scrapers for cleaning the aquarium glass, one or two 3- to 5-gallon plastic buckets, a gravel siphon, a small net for catching and moving fish and removing large debris, and perhaps plant tongs and small

pots for planting purposes. A few plant food tablets would also be worthwhile.

SETTING UP THE DISPLAY

Setting up your display can take quite a while, so do this only when you have plenty of time. It is useful to make a sketch of where you plan to feature major decorations such as large rocks and driftwood, because it is easier to move these around on paper rather than in the tank! When this is done, first of all prepare some water in buckets and allow it to stand overnight in the room of the aquarium. This will bring it to room temperature. Test it for chlorine, as well as for its pH, hardness, and other compounds as discussed in an earlier chapter. Make notes of your readings so that you have baseline readings to compare your aquarium water to later on.

Have everything at hand when you commence setting up. Place the tank on its stand and double check that it is very secure. If an undergravel filter is to be used, this must be placed in first. Be sure it's a snug fit; otherwise, water will bypass the main body of the filter and exit via gaps, taking the path of least resistance.

The gravel goes in next. If you wish to create a stepped effect you can use strips of plastic glued to a plastic base to act as retainers for terraces, or you can purchase "walls" from your pet dealer, or use slate or other flat rocks to act as retainers. The ultimate depth of the gravel will range from about one inch in the foreground to 2-3 inches at the sides and rear. By this arrangement, debris and mulm is encouraged to fall toward the front of the tank or terraces, where it is more easily removed.

Before the gravel has reached its full depth, insert the rocks and other decorations. Be sure they are well anchored so that there are no pockets where food could accumulate and decay. Build up around these. The heater and filter tubes can now be placed into position and disguised behind rocks, or placed where they will be hidden by plants.

At this point some water can be poured or siphoned from a bucket into the tank. Let it flow gently onto a saucer, or a piece of cardboard, so as not to disturb the gravel. Now is the time to insert plants, either in small pots or directly into the gravel. The advantage of planting at this time is that the leaves will float on the water and not be in your way, nor will you be trying to plant them in deep water.

With everything in place you can now half-fill the aquarium and assess it. If all is well, finish filling the tank to about one inch below its capacity. Add the hood and power up the filter and heater. (Be sure nothing is plugged into sockets while your hands are in the water!) In order for biological action to commence quickly, you can purchase starter cultures from your pet shop. It takes time for aerobic bacteria to colonize the gravel bed, and thus start the nitrogen cycle. Likewise, plants need time to take root.

During the next week or so you should take regular pH and other readings, as well as see that the heater and filter are operating correctly. Any dying leaves on plants should be removed. Only when all the conditions are satisfactory, and stable(!) should the first guppies be introduced.

Stocking the Aquarium

Initially, you need only two or three guppies, and these should be very healthy individuals. Transport them home as quickly as possible so that the water in their plastic bag does not cool and cause stress. The bag should be floated on the water surface for a few minutes so temperature equalization can take place. Add some tank water to the bag. When you are ready to release the fish, open the neck of the bag and let the guppies gently swim out. The next few days will tell you if the initial inhabitants have settled in and are doing well, in which case you can then start to add more stock—but never stock up too rapidly and risk upsetting the delicate balance that should be taking place. Ideally, after the initial fish have been placed in the aquarium, all further stock should be quarantined as a precaution. This is discussed further in the health chapter.

From here on in it is a matter of making partial water changes, doing routine cleaning and replacement of filter media, and generally keeping the aquarium clean. Of course, observation of your fish is paramount in order that you can quickly spot any that might be acting abnormally.

FEEDING

Compared with the situation that prevailed for aquarists of only about thirty years ago, the present-day hobbyist is absolutely spoiled when it comes to commercially prepared fish foods. There is no longer the need to be trying to rear cultures of live foods that are both messy and rather smelly (although some of the best guppy breeders still do). Vast sums of money have been invested into fish nutrition in order to cater for the needs of the millions of hobbyists worldwide.

FEEDING TYPES

All fish species have evolved to eat certain types of foods, and this is reflected in a number of ways. For example, the guppy has a relatively long digestive tract. This tells us that it eats quite a bit of plant matter, which needs a longer period of digestion than does animal protein in order to be broken down to its basic ingredients. The guppy's upturned mouth indicates it has evolved to be a surface feeder, and that it snatches live foods that alight on the surface. In other words, its diet is a mixture of live foods and plant matter. Such feeding types are called *omnivorous*, as compared to those that are *carnivorous* (predominately flesh eaters) and those which are *herbivorous* (predominately plant eaters). Young guppies are situated more toward the carnivorous end of the omnivore scale. They need to put on body weight quickly, and proteins are the best way of doing

One of Gan's best selling guppies is this redtail guppy which are produced in Singapore at the Gan Aquarium Fish Farm.

this. As they mature they need fewer proteins and more carbohydrates. The latter are the most readily available and easily acquired sources of energy for general day-to-day muscular activity.

From the feeding type, conclusions can be drawn as to feeding habits. Carnivores are able to gorge on a meal, then be relatively inactive while the food is metabolized. Herbivores need to graze steadily in order that there is a flow of food at all times in their digestive tract. The omnivore is somewhere between these two. Translated into feeding regimens, an omnivore is best fed about three times a day: morning, afternoon, and early evening (before the aquarium lights are switched off). If any of the meals

must be omitted because of your schedule, the afternoon one would be the best. Young fry do, of course, need more meals per day if maximum growth is to be achieved.

FOOD FORMS

The form in which you provide food to your guppies probably will fall into one of the following categories: flake, tablet, powdered, liquid, freeze-dried, frozen, fresh, and live.

Flake: This is probably the most popular form and is available in a range of ingredient bases, ranging from wholly vegetable to high-protein, and from slow- to fast-sinking to suit the feeding preferences of different species. Extra care must be used when feeding flake foods because they

The red snakeskin guppy produced by Gan Aquarium Fish Farm.

PHOTO BY CHEW KENG LOON.

PHOTO BY CHEW KENG LOON.

The famous Blond Tuxedo Guppy produced by Gan Aquarium Fish Farm in Singapore.

can easily fall into crevices if uneaten, then decay, to the detriment of water quality. Little and often is the best way to use them.

Tablet: These can either be free-falling, or stuck to the aquarium glass. One advantage of foods placed in set positions is that you can encourage your guppies to feed at given locations. You are then better able to observe their individual feeding habits, and are more likely to notice if any are missing at feeding time—which would prompt you to wonder why.

Powdered: In this form the food is more scattered throughout the aquarium and better suited to very small fry. As with flake food, a little and often is the best method to avoid the risk of polluting the water.

Liquid: These foods are also well suited to very young fry and will find their way, via the water circulation, to those areas of the tank where youngsters may be taking refuge. They are quickly eaten and digested.

Freeze-dried: These are popular and enable high-protein foods (such as tubifex worms) to be fed without the risk of introducing pathogens. They store well and swell as they absorb water.

Frozen: Almost as "hygienic" as freeze-dried, they are the obvious alternative to live foods with respect to the nutritional ingredients they possess. They allow you to feed many foods that ordinarily would either not be readily available to you, or are seasonal.

Fresh: This term is used to

embrace the many foods you can supply from your home kitchen. Examples are fresh vegetables, cheese, and other dairy byproducts, boiled egg, minced lean meats, fruit, cereal, and their byproducts. Of course, these must be presented in a form that can be eaten by guppies. They can be minced, then formed into cubes held together by gelatin, or they can be crushed until very small and offered as is, or they can be passed through a blender and given as a mixed solution. Slivers of meat can be suspended in the aquarium to be nibbled on for short periods, so there are numerous ways these foods can be offered to your guppies. Be cautious, however, as many of these foods will foul the water quickly if uneaten.

Live foods: These include worms (grindal, white, tubifex, earth) of various types and sizes, insects, fish eggs, daphnia, and brine shrimp, to name but a few. Again, some are already very small and so can be fed as they are, but others will needed chopping to an acceptable size. If this does not appeal to you, the answer is to purchase them in the frozen state.

If live foods are caught from natural waters, be aware that they can introduce pathogens into your aquarium, as well as the larvae of insects that may be predatory on guppies.

OVERFEEDING

One of the great dangers for any aquarist, but especially for those new to the hobby, is overfeeding. With guppies and other fishes you simply cannot casually drop a quantity of food into the water on the basis that what is not eaten can be removed sometime later

The so-called Gan Dragon Head Guppy.

PHOTO BY CHEW KENG LOON.

The blue variegated guppy strain produced by the Gan Aquarium Fish Farm in Singapore.

and discarded, as sometimes can be done with mammals, birds, and other land creatures. The situation is made even more problematic because even excessive quantities of food will still appear to us to be a relatively small amount. But that small amount, on a progressive basis and in a small closed system, which is what an aquarium is, can soon have a dramatic effect on the quality of the water. It can result in an increasing pollution rate that the filter system and plants cannot cope with. Your fish (and plants) will become sickly and soon perish.

The remedy is to always watch your fish at feeding time. Place only a very small amount of food in the water and observe how quickly it is all eaten. You can always give a little extra, but you cannot as easily remove the

excess. As a guide, the fish should devour most of the food within 2-3 minutes. Small but numerous meals are your best policy initially. In a mature, well-planted tank, your fish will rarely be at risk to starvation. There will always be microorganisms living on the substrate, the plants, and the decorations. Regular siphoning of the substrate, coupled with partial water changes and checks on the pH and nitrite levels, are your means to ensure that pollution is never a problem. Guppies are hardy and extremely easy fish to care for, but this does not mean that a casual approach will suffice.

FEED A BALANCED DIET

Fishes are no different than other animals in that they need a well-balanced diet if they are to

PHOTO BY CHEW KENG LOON.

This neon guppy category entry took Third Prize at the Aquarama '93 Guppy Show held in Singapore.

reach optimum size, retain full breeding vigor, and display their colors and fins to best effect. *Balanced* means receiving the required amounts of proteins, carbohydrates, fats, vitamins, and minerals, and in the proper ratios. Achieving balance is not easy because so many factors are involved. Every aquarium is quite unique—even two in the same room are different micro-worlds.

As you gain practical experience you will, by observation, results, and reading, learn more about *balance.* Initially, proceed by ensuring that you supply a wide range of foods in various forms. Do not assume that all commercial foods are complete diets. Read the labels.

By supplying a range of foods you minimize the possibility that some important ingredient is lacking in the diet of your fish. Make feeding an integral part of your husbandry and the results will more than justify the effort.

Winners of the Second Prize in the 1993 Aquarama were these tuxedo guppies.

PHOTO BY CHEW KENG LOON.

GUPPY VARIETIES

Guppies may be compared to the most majestic of coldwater fishes—koi—in that while they are seen in a number of recognized varieties, the potential colors and patterns are limitless. New strains continually are being created, and new mutations that may be worthy of selective development appear spontaneously. So, whether you want a particular variety, or just a collection of dazzling-looking fish for your display tank, you have started with the right species.

In this chapter we can only take a brief look at the more obvious fin shapes and color patterns, but these will give you a good idea just what an array of forms there are. It should also be mentioned that, compared to the early years of this hobby, even females can be obtained today in some very pretty color and fin combinations.

When breeding guppies you will find that the mating of two comparable types will not normally produce 100% of the same type and color. This is because very many gene combinations go into producing patterns, colors, and fin shapes. As a consequence, the random way in which genes reassemble themselves at fertilization is such that totally purebreeding varieties are the exception rather than the rule. Dominant genes will, of course, express themselves, but it is the hidden recessives that may come together to create colors,

patterns, and fin shapes that might not have been anticipated based on the appearance of the parents. This is a double-edged sword. It creates enormous problems for the specialty breeder, yet may be greatly appreciated by the average fancier, who looks forward to each brood in anticipation of the array of colors and forms that may be produced.

FINS

There are at least twelve fin shapes to choose from. Some are very obvious, their name making their shapes easily recognizable. Others are not so easily identified and can be mistaken for other shapes. Indeed, the names themselves have changed in some instances, or the same fin shape is known by different names in different areas or countries. These shapes are determined from male guppies; females usually have tails that are rounded, or at least less developed than those of the males.

1) **Deltatail:** A very popular variety, the deltatail exhibits a wide triangular shape that, more than any other, allows the beautiful colors and patterns seen in guppies to be displayed at their very best. Its drawback is that as the guppy ages the thin edges start to break. Also, the tail can be ruined if any of the tank inhabitants are fin nippers.

Red Blond Deltatail developed at the Gan Aquarium Fish Farm.

A blue variegated longfin developed by Gan Aquarium Fish Farm.

The Gan White Diamond longfin guppy.

2) **Longfin:** This is a variation on the deltatail in which some of the fin rays of the tail grow longer.

3) **Fantail:** Another of the broadtail group, this is not as wide as the deltatail, but has more gently curving upper and lower edges.

4) **Veiltail:** This is a wide-tailed variety similar to the deltatail, but not as large.

5) **Ribbontail:** As the name suggests, the upper and lower edges of this shape are more parallel than in the deltatail shapes. Also called the flagtail, bannertail, or scarftail by some hobbyists.

6) **Double Swordtail:** In this popular variety the upper and lower fin lobes are extended like rapiers. If only the upper lobe is extended it is known as a top swordtail, if only the lower lobe it is a bottom swordtail.

The double swordtail guppy developed by Gan.

7) **Spadetail:** Self -explanatory; like the ace of spades.

8) **Roundtail:** This is the basic shape of the wild guppy tail and is basically a spadetail without the point.

9) **Pointed Tail:** This is a

The variegated gold guppy produced at the Gan Aquarium Fish Hatchery.

The Japanese ribbontail produced and photographed by Tanaka.

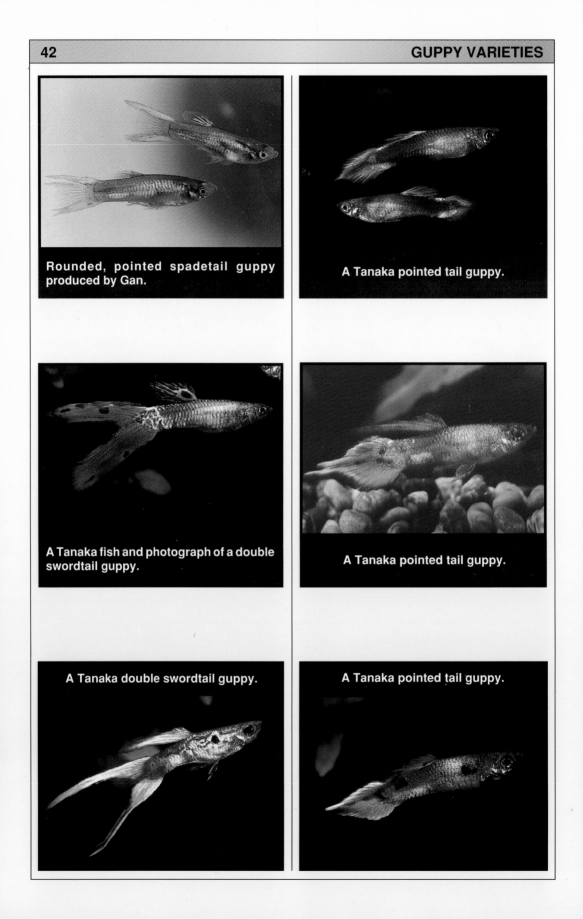

Rounded, pointed spadetail guppy produced by Gan.

A Tanaka pointed tail guppy.

A Tanaka fish and photograph of a double swordtail guppy.

A Tanaka pointed tail guppy.

A Tanaka double swordtail guppy.

A Tanaka pointed tail guppy.

A Tanaka pintail or lacetail.

A Green Diamond Roundtail produced by Gan.

A snakeskin lace produced by Tanaka.

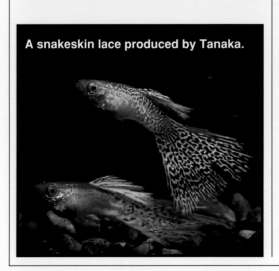

roundtail, but with a central pointed extension to it. Also called a pintail.

12) **Lacetail:** This is rather like the pintail, but the extension is much shorter. Speartail is perhaps a better descriptive term.

PATTERNS

As with the tail fin, only much more so, the number of names applied to color patterns is tremendous. Specialty breeders will apply their own names to particular variations of a pattern they believe to be representative of their stock. However, the following are the basic major genetic variations.

Mosaic: In this pattern, which is one based on the tail fin, though today it can also be seen in the dorsal, there are irregular blotches of color radiating from the caudal peduncle, which is a dark blue color. When the dark blotches are nicely dispersed the effect is quite beautiful, but when they coalesce, or are all toward one side of the tail, the effect is far less striking. There are many variations of the mosaic in numerous color combinations, though the fiery orange-red ground color with black markings is one of the perennial favorites.

Grass: This pattern also was originally restricted to the caudal fin, but also may now be seen in the dorsal. It is a pattern in which the dark markings again radiate from the peduncle, but unlike those of the mosaic, they are fine, and often composed of many small spots in a straight line. The "glass grass" guppy has the spots

A Tanaka mosaic guppy.

A Tanaka mosaic guppy.

A Tanaka glass leopard guppy.

and fine lines against an almost transparent ground color. The leopard is a very striking pattern in which the markings are reminiscent of those on a leopard. As with mosaics, the grass patterns come in a range of colors, including black, blue, yellow, green, and of course, red. Although the body colors of fish with these patterns can also be very pretty, they look quite plain next to the brilliance of the tail and dorsal fins.

Cobra: Also called the king cobra or snakeskin, this is a body pattern in which there are unbroken lines of pigment that interconnect in a snakeskin pattern. Sometimes the lines break up too much, or they are more striped than snakeskin-like, but even these can still look very impressive. The cobra is available with any of the tail shapes, patterns and colors; thus, a very stunning fish is possible. When these variations are brought together in the same guppy you can image the potential for naming them!

A variation on the cobra pattern is that called the "tiger." As you may deduce, this pattern results in vertical bars of dark pigment on a lighter background that produces a tiger-striped effect.

Tuxedo: As the name suggests, this variety has half the body in black, the other half in any other color. The black may begin just ahead of or behind the dorsal fin, and extends to the end of the caudal peduncle. While a neat vertical line of demarcation between the black and the other

PHOTO BY MP & C PIEDNOIR.

A European snakeskin guppy.

The most popular and productive of Japanese fish breeders is Tanaka. This is the Tanaka Tuxedo.

colors is desirable, this is only seen in the most outstanding of individuals. The variety is also known as the half-black. As with all patterns, the tuxedo is available in a range of colors, and some, such as the blue, are very impressive. It has a blue body followed by the black tuxedo, then blue in the caudal and dorsal fins, with the caudal being edged in black. The flamingo is a red fish with a black tuxedo; again, this is a guppy to behold if it is a good specimen.

The tuxedo pattern is a dominant mutation and can be combined with other patterns on the forebody, as well as with the various fin shapes and patterns.

There are many color combinations that can be seen on guppy bodies, but if you concentrate your attention on the main features discussed in this chapter you will not be at a loss to understand which basic variety you are looking at.

This wonderful guppy is a golden red tuxedo with a long, flowing dorsal with a small slit in the tail.

PHOTO BY HANS JOACHIM RICHTER.

BREEDING STRATEGY

It would be quite impossible to discuss the genetics of the guppy in a small chapter, so we will review basic breeding strategy and introduce you to simple genetics using examples seen in the guppy.

BREEDING OBJECTIVES

Whenever two animals are mated under domestic conditions, there should be definite objectives that are beyond the simple act of perpetuating the species. It requires no skill to simply have guppies breed, but breeding to produce superior fish with very fixed qualities of color, finnage, and vigor is another matter. This requires great dedication, detailed record-keeping, the ability to make sound judgments based on results, and, it must always be added, a degree of luck in the way the random nature of genes work for you in a program.

The prime objectives of any breeder must always be good health and breeding vigor. You will assuredly be faced with a need to compromise between health and desired characteristics, but never allow this to happen unless you are quite sure there really is no other option. Thereafter, rapidly make health the priority once you have achieved your characteristic objective.

LIMIT YOUR AMBITIONS

As an ambitious breeder, you will want to achieve many things all at once. You may wish to improve the fins and the colors, as well as keep examples of the many varieties. As tempting as this may be, the more numerous your desires, the less likely it will be that success will be achieved in any one area, such as color, fins, vigor, or conformation. Once you understand the basics of genetics, you will appreciate just why this comment is so true, especially when it concerns the large number of offspring that would be involved.

It is always best, even if you keep a number of varieties in a display tank, to concentrate your breeding program on a limited number of objectives. But remember that if you do keep a mixed-variety display tank you must not use the female fish from that tank for breeding; otherwise, there would be little point in specialized breeding. Remember that female guppies are able to store sperm that can be used to fertilize numerous broods of fry. You'll never be able to be sure of the father unless you mate a virgin female with one male. This factor alone makes planned guppy breeding more complicated than it is with most other animals.

ACHIEVING OBJECTIVES

There are two ways in which you can go about improving your guppies. One is by assessing a number of features together, then selecting from those fish that meet your overall standard. The other is to concentrate on one or two features at a time, then concentrate on other features only when the desired result in the former is achieved. Progress is slower in any one feature when you are dealing with a number of features than when you concentrate on one or two. But in the long term, either option achieves your objectives.

When tandem breeding (one feature at a time) is the method used, you must always be careful that, in moving your priorities to the next feature, undue deterioration in the standard of the feature that has already been improved is not a consequence. To limit the possibility of this happening necessitates a "closed" breeding program.

THE CLOSED PROGRAM

The meaning of a closed program is that, having obtained stock of an acceptable standard, you do not continue to use stock from outside sources when its genotype is unknown, and which could therefore hinder the progress of your entire program. Out of necessity, a closed program means you will be inbreeding to some degree. This latter term often is wrongly associated with negatives in the average beginner's mind, so let's apply a definition to it. It is the mating of individuals from the same line: offspring-to-parent, brother-to-sister, etc. In reality, it would be impossible to establish and improve a variety of a species without an inbreeding policy.

There are potential negatives when inbreeding. These can only be overcome by rigorous culling of

breeding stock at each generation, but this fact applies to any form of breeding if improvements are to be achieved.

BASIC GENETIC THEORY

You cannot be a serious breeder of guppies unless you understand the basics of how the features you wish to deal with are passed from one generation to the next. You must therefore learn about genetics to at least the level that you can achieve your objectives and avoid pitfalls.

Genes are sequences of DNA that code for a particular trait. Genes are attached to larger structures called *chromosomes*. Some genes act in a major manner in that their presence in a single dose is sufficient to change a feature. Others require two genes to achieve this. Still others work on an additive basis, and the features they control are said to be *polygenic* in transmission. Color and fins are examples of the first two types, size being an example of polygenic action.

Although color and fins are controlled by major gene action, they are also subject to polygenes in the form of those that modify the depth of color or size of fins. These are aptly called *modifier genes*. Another influence over color and fins you will need to be aware of is that of the guppy's sex. Features that are related to the sex of an animal are known as *sex-linked*. These obviously include matters such as physical and physiological differences between the sexes. A few colors and fin types are also subject to sex genes, as compared to most others that are inherited regardless of which sex happens to carry them.

HOW GENES WORK

The chromosomes already mentioned are found in pairs within the body cells. The exception is in the reproductive cells (sex cells). In the guppy (and humans, as well), the chromosomes of the female are designated **XX**, those of the male **XY**.

On the chromosomes, each gene's position is known as its *locus.* On the opposite chromosome of a pair there is a similar locus for that feature. Thus, with respect to a simple color, such as blue, albino, or gold, two genes determine the color, one on each chromosome of a pair at the same locus. When guppies mate, their paired chromosomes separate. Each goes into a sex cell, so that each sex cell contains one of the original chromosomes (thus half the genes) that determined the color and other features of the parent. The sex cells contain one each of all the paired autosomal chromosomes, plus either an X or Y chromosome.

When the sex cells (egg and sperm) unite at fertilization, the paired chromosomes (thus genes) are reestablished. The process is rather more complex than this as far as the genes go, but in essence this is what happens. If the genes of both parents at the same locus are identical or nearly so, the offspring will express that trait in the same manner as both parents. More often, the genes are a little different, and the genetic recombination may create a new expression of a trait in the offspring. Let us look at this more carefully so you will understand.

A grand champion Blond Diamond Roundtail guppy produced by Gan Aquarium Fish Farm.

If a given gene determines that a guppy will have a wild coloration, then if both genes of a pair (one from each parent) are for this expression, it will have wild coloration. If this individual mates with one of a similar type, the only combination of their union will be the wild type. We can show this mating by using letters to represent the genes, which is how you will work out the results of different matings.

There is a major gene that allows all other color genes to express themselves. It is designated as **C,** meaning full color (wild type gene). A wild guppy thus has two **C** genes (one on each chromosome of a pair). If two similar wild-type guppies mate, the formula will be **CC** x **CC** = **CC.** No other combination of genes is possible.

MUTATIONS

A mutation is said to have taken place when there is a change in the way a gene expresses itself. Something happens that alters the chemical makeup of the gene. It remains at its locus, and creates an

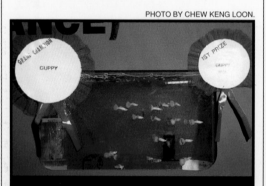

PHOTO BY CHEW KENG LOON.

This tankful of identical guppies won First Prize and Grand Champion in the Neon Guppy Category at the Aquarama '93. Fish produced at the Gan Aquarium Fish Hatchery.

alternative expression to the normal situation (wild type) at that locus. The gene may have variable powers of expression, but three in particular are of interest to us at this level of study.

A *dominant* gene is one that can express itself when present in single dose (just one gene of a pair at a given locus). A *recessive* gene is one that must be present in double dose (both genes of a pair) to be seen in the offspring. When one of each type is present the dominant gene will be seen, but the recessive is still there. It cannot express itself because it is masked by the more potent dominant. However, it retains its own identity, and can be transmitted just as the dominant can. They both have an equal chance of being passed on to their progeny.

The third type of gene expression is known as *incomplete dominance.* In this, the dominant gene is not able to fully suppress the recessive gene. As a result, the fish may display both gene expressions in the same fish, or an apparent blending between the two types (a light and dark blue, for example). Genes never truly blend, so if they appear to do so it is because of incomplete dominance, or because another pair of genes is affecting them (as is the case with the veiltail variety).

The dominant gene is represented by a capital letter, the recessive by a lowercase letter. The mutational gene is always given the same letter as its dominant alternative. This is so you do not lose sight of the fact that one is the alternative (called an *allelomorph*) of the other. When a pair of genes are for the same expression of a trait, the feature they determine is said to be *homozygous* = purebreeding. When they are for differing expressions the feature is *heterozygous* = non-purebreeding.

CALCULATING EXPECTATIONS

The foregoing provides you with some basic knowledge of genes, so now we can consider how to work out expectations from given pairings. We'll begin with albinism, which is inherited in a simple recessive manner. However, in some fishes, including guppies, albinism is incomplete. By this is meant that it does not suppress all pigments, only the melanins that create black and brown.

In point of fact, many mutations in guppies confound the expectations of genetics, but this does not negate their importance. It is simply that in these and other fishes the mode of transmission is very complex, and still not fully understood for some varieties. But you can be assured that all colors are inherited in a way that follows the rules of inheritance.

A pure wild-colored guppy has the genotype **CC,** while the albino variant is **cc.** If a **CC** fish is paired with a **cc** fish, the wild type can pass only a **C** gene to its offspring, and the albino can only pass on a **c** for its contribution. This is the only potential combination of these two genes, so all the offspring must have the genotype **Cc.** Full color is dominant to albinism, so the first generation all have wild type coloration. They are wild (or normals), heterozygous for albinism. We can now differentiate between two types of normal coloration. The one phenotype (appearance) can result from two quite different genotypes (homozygous **CC** and heterozygous **Cc).** If the heterozygous offspring are inbred to each other we will produce some albinos and some normals. In order to work these out for yourself in other simple recessive mutations, you must calculate every potential combination of the

genes each parent could pass to their fry. In this particular mating of brother to sister the formula would be: **Cc** x **Cc = CC, Cc, Cc, cc.** In other words, 25% will be homozygous normal, 50% will be heterozygous normal, and 25% will be albino (homozygous recessive). This means that 75% will look

PHOTO BY TANAKA.

With many guppies, getting fish to look alike does not mean that they are identical but that they can be recognized as a strain.

normal and 25% will be albino. The only way you can establish which of the wild types are purebreeding (homozygous) is by further matings.

The calculation gives us a theoretical expectation ratio of combinations. These will work out over the long run, though not necessarily a short run (such as one particular brood). This is because they are subject to random selection—much as is the case if you flip a coin. There will be a 50/50 split of heads or tails if you do an infinite number of coin flips, but over the short run some variations are possible. For instance, you could throw three or four heads in a row.

Note that a dominantly controlled feature can be split for a recessive gene, but a recessive feature cannot be split if it is visible in the individual. In other words, a mating of two albinos produces only albinos. Writing the genotype of a split guppy is done thus: Normal/albino—that in front of the slash is visible (dominant), that behind it is masked (recessive). In writing the genotype of the **CC** or **Cc** offspring produced in the sibling mating, this is done as **C-.**

PHOTO AND FISH BY TANAKA.

This exceptionally beautiful strain is a Leopard/Tiger with a new kind of tail.

The dash indicates that the second gene is unknown and could be either **C** or **c.** In using the albino as an example of simple gene action involving recessive mutations I must add an important footnote. While the 3:1 ratio is typical of such a mating when breeding two heterozygotes, this assumes that there are no secondary problems that affect the expectations. In the albino guppy there are such complications. The actual results are more likely to be on the order of 53:1 wild to albino. This is because the albino gene in these fish is linked to an inherent weakness, or lethal recessive gene, that results in a very high death rate of albino fry before they are born.

MORE COMPLEX MATINGS

In the foregoing matings we considered only one color locus, that being the one controlling full color. But there are many others. When two loci are involved things are more complex, and even more so when three or more loci are considered. As you increase the number of loci under consideration, so you dramatically increase the number of potential permutations. We will look only at a mating involving two mutations, as this will illustrate what you must do.

Let us pair a blue guppy (genotype **rr**) with an albino, (genotype **cc**). When doing this it is most important that you do not forget to include the full genotype of the individuals, for reasons that will soon become apparent. The blue guppy is actually **CCrr**, while the albino is **ccRR**. Remember, we are now dealing with two loci, that for albino and that for blue. At the albino (full color) locus the blue is normal (non-albino), the albino being normal (non-blue) at the blue locus.

The blue guppy can pass on only a blue gene at the blue locus and a normal gene at the full color locus. It therefore passes the genes **C** and **r** on to its offspring. The albino can pass on only a **c** gene at the full color locus and only an **R** at the blue locus. It thus passes on **c** and **R.** The genotype of the first generation is therefore **CcRr.** Translated into color, all the offspring are normal-looking (wild type), but are heterozygous for both blue and albino.

If these youngsters are inbred

the color ratio expectations are:

9 Normals—1 homozygous (**CCRR**), 2 Normal/blue (**CCRr**), 4 Normal/albino & blue (**CcRr**), 2 Normal/albino (**CcRR**).

3 Blue comprising the following genotypes:

    1 Homozygous (**CCrr**)
    2 Blue/albino (**CcRR**)

3 Albino comprising the following genotypes:

    1 Homozygous (**ccRR**)
    2 Albino/blue (**ccRr**)

1 Albino Blue (Homozygous for both colors) (**ccrr**)

In order to minimize the risk of error in making calculations involving two or more mutations it is wise to use a checkerboard-like arrangement called a Punnett square. The genes that each parent can pass are placed along the horizontal and vertical planes. It is then a simple matter to fill in the blank squares.

SEX LINKAGE

The guppy has 22 pairs of autosomal (body) chromosomes and one pair of sex chromosomes. Most features of the fish are carried on the autosomes, but some, including certain colors and fin types, are carried on the sex chromosomes. With autosomal genes it does matter which sex carries the mutations. This is not the case with sex-linked genes.

This aspect of genetics often confounds the beginner. But it is actually quite simple as long as you always bear in mind which sex chromosome is linked to which feature. If a feature is carried on the **X** chromosome then it can be passed to both daughters and

sons, but if it is on the **Y** chromosome only the males can inherit it. In guppies the mutant dark posterior body and caudal peduncle color is known as *nigrocaudatus* or *tuxedo* (**N^t**), and is carried on the **X** chromosome, while the iridescent color pattern in this same area is carried on the **Y** chromosome. The mutations are both dominant. If no tuxedo is present, the **X** chromosome will have the genotype of **XN**, which is shown in some texts as **Ch**,

PHOTO BY CHEW KENG LOON.

The Rainbow Guppy category winner, First Prize in Aquarama '93.

meaning caudal hyaline or transparent. The use of differing letters for the same locus can cause confusion, so I have used the same letters, as in the rest of this text, for alleles at a locus. The **N** gene is the normal wild type (non-tuxedo) dominant. However, the tuxedo gene is dominant to the wild type. This is indicated by the superscripted "**t**" that indicates it is a mutational gene.

Let us pair a tuxedo female of

$XN^t XN^t$ genotype with a male iridescent which caries no tuxedo mutant, so has a genotype of $XN YI^p$, where the superscript "p" indicates the mutant iridescent pattern and "**I**" is normal wild type (non-iridescent). Only two permutations are possible from this union.

1) The XN^t tuxedo gene of the female can combine with the non-tuxedo gene of the male to create $XN^t XN$. This creates tuxedo females heterozygous for non-tuxedo.

2) The XN^t of the female can combine with the YI^p of the male to create $XN^t YI^p$, which is a tuxedo

PHOTO AND FISH BY TANAKA.

The huge spots in the tails of these two guppies indicate they are closely related and a genetic variation.

iridescent male. However, the tuxedo gene is superdominant when combined with the dominant iridescent and results in masking its presence. It is said to be *epistatic* to iridescent. That the I^p gene is present we will now prove. We will mate the male ($XN^t YI^p$) with a female tuxedo, but which is heterozygous for non-tuxedo. Her genotype is thus $XN^t XN$. The four potential permutations are:

1) $XN^t XN^t$ = Homozygous tuxedo females;

2) $XN^t XN$ = Tuxedo females split for non tuxedo;

3) $XN^t YI^p$ = Tuxedo masking iridescent males;

4) $XNYI^p$ = Iridescent males.

As the female cannot carry the iridescent gene the males displaying this color (4) must have inherited the gene from their father, even though it was not visible in him due to the presence of the tuxedo gene. Permutation (3) also carries this mutant gene, but is exactly like his father in appearance.

Other genes that are carried on the sex chromosomes include the veiltail, double swordtail (**Y** chromosome) and flavus (yellow-tailed: **X** chromosome). The veiltail is interesting because it results from the interaction of the flavus and double-sword mutant, which are on different sex chromosomes.

From the foregoing you will appreciate that breeding for varieties is a complicated undertaking, for what is discussed here is only the bare bones of guppy genetics. However, it should acquaint you with the most-used terminology. With this knowledge understood, you are now ready to tackle more detailed texts on this subject.

PRACTICAL BREEDING

Although guppies are extremely easy to breed, there are a number of pitfalls that make them very difficult if the object is to be selective with regard to colors and fin shapes. Furthermore, you also must provide safety for the newborn fry; otherwise, their mother, and any other fishes near them (as in a community tank), will take delight in consuming them as a tasty snack.

The major problem confronting the breeder who wishes to breed for certain colors and fin shapes is that the female can store sperm from a given mating and use these to fertilize up to four or more additional broods. This fact alone can play havoc with the serious breeder's program, and is the main reason why there are so many "mongrel" guppies to be seen. If the sexes are not separated at the earliest possible time, the likelihood is that the young males will mate with their mother, their sisters, and any other willing females in the aquarium! With this fact in mind we must first consider the basic breeding life of the two sexes.

GUPPY BREEDING LIFE CYCLE

The guppy has an average lifespan of 12 months, somewhat less in strains that have resulted from a program in which breeding vigor has been sacrificed at the expense of purely esthetic qualities (color pattern, fin size and shape). Clearly, in such a short time, and given the sperm-storing capacity of the female, much, perhaps all of her breeding life could easily be wasted if she should be mated by an undesirable male. You must wait until she has used up all the sperm packets before she can then be mated to the desired male. Unfortunately, you cannot tell when this has happened, and most breeders consider such a female lost to further breeding.

The breeding life cycle can be broadly divided into the following time frames:

Birth to 4 weeks: This is the period in which the gonopodium develops in the male. Once this is complete he can mate. This is the time when the sexes must be separated.

PHOTOS AND FISH BY TANAKA.

What beauty in these guppies; not only are they similarly colored but their tails are almost as long as their bodies.

5-9 weeks: During this period the colors really start to show themselves and the fins are getting larger. The sexes must have been separated by the early part of this period if virgin females are to be obtained.

10-26 weeks: This is the time when the guppy is at its most beautiful, and when maximum breeding capacity is reached. Shortly after the start of this period the female suddenly increases her size compared to the male.

27 weeks onward: Now very mature, the colors and breeding capacity start to recede, the more so if water conditions are not ideal.

free-swimming youngster is about 28 days. It can be shorter or much longer depending on the strain, the individual parents, and the environmental conditions, food, and especially the water temperature. As the female gets near to the time of spawning her abdomen will swell. You will see the typical dark or gravid spot at the rear of the abdomen that indicates fetal development. The heads of the fry may be seen through the abdominal wall in the gravid spot shortly before they are actually born.

PHOTO BY DR. HERBERT R. AXELROD.

You can see the unborn fry through the translucent belly of the female guppy.

THE BREEDING TANK

You will need a number of small breeding tanks of 10-gallon capacity. The female will need to be kept in one of these, while at least two more will be required to house the youngsters once they are old enough to be separated into single-sex groups. The more guppies you breed in terms of numbers or strains, the more tanks you will need. This is why it is wise to specialize in just one variety, and also to commence with a small program and let it expand slowly according to your interest and available cash. It is

BROOD SIZE

The first brood is normally of about 10 fry. Subsequent broods increase in number within the range of 20-100, though 25-40 is perhaps typical. The factors that influence brood size are the strain of guppy, its breeding vigor, and the conditions under which it has been kept with regard to temperature and water quality.

INCUBATION

The time it takes the fertilized egg to develop and be born as a very easy for the beginner to become overwhelmed by an over-ambitious program.

The tank should be freshly prepared for each breeding. It should be well-planted and contain a heater and a simple sponge or box filter. Mating will take place quickly because the male guppy normally has strong procreative desires. After a few days the male can be removed so he does not cause stress to the female by habitually chasing her around the tank.

BREEDING TRAPS

You will need a breeding trap in the tank in order to provide safety for the newly born fry. A number of models are made commercially. The trap is essentially a small cage in which the female is housed as she nears term. Its sides have small openings large enough for the fry to swim through, but too small for the female. If it is large enough to house a few strands of floating plants, so much the better, as this will help relax the female. Do not place her in the trap too early, as she may become overstressed and abort her brood. A few days before she is due to give birth you can

This strain of boldly marked guppies has disappeared from the domestic scene. If they reappear, be sure to get some as they produce very highly colored guppies. Photo by Tanaka who developed these fish.

raise the temperature by 2-3°F: this will encourage her to have her babies.

REARING THE FRY

Young fry need to be able to feed on a continuous basis, and making this so in the first days of their lives is particularly vital. The nauplii of brine shrimp (*Artemia salina*) are an excellent food; brine shrimp eggs and the directions for hatching them can be obtained from your pet shop. Prepared fry foods also are available in liquid, powder, or micro-flake forms. If the fry are underfed the larger, more aggressive youngsters will soon devour the more timid individuals because the latter will not have received their share of the food. If you have utilized a good-sized breeding tank it is now that it will pay dividends, especially if it is well-planted. The more space the fish have, the better they will grow. A large rearing tank also avoids the need to relocate the fry until they are ready to be sex-grouped. Moving any fish from one environment to another is always stressful, all the more so for youngsters.

QUALITY CULLING

It is very important that from the time they are born until they are mature you remove any individuals that display deformities of any kind—those with incorrect physical conformation, poor fins, and an inability to swim correctly. As the fish mature you will be selecting for quality of fin and color pattern, so that ultimately you will retain only a very few fish for onward breeding. Most breeders opt to use the culls as feeder fish for larger, predatory fishes such as cichlids.

Clearly, once the young virgin females have been separated from the males you cannot place them into a community of guppies or other fishes. They should be given their own tank until they are ready to be bred at about four months of age. Once their breeding life is over they can be placed in the community tank, because their smaller litters will be unlikely to survive in this location.

From the foregoing you will appreciate that serious breeding of guppies is not as easy as you may have at first thought. You are always confronted with the problem of keeping females from casual matings. If you stay with one variety, then at least in the event unwanted matings take place you will still have a recognizable variety from such matings.

An old strain of bronze guppies was utilized to prepare this un-named Japanese strain produced and photographed by Tanaka.

MAINTAINING GOOD HEALTH

Guppies are very hardy little fish, but their small size does mean that if they contract a problem they can very rapidly deteriorate and die. When a fish does develop a condition or disease the added problem is that all other fish sharing the same water will of course be exposed to it. The cliché that prevention is nine-tenths of a cure is very true where fishes, especially guppies, are concerned.

Once one or more fish have become ill you are confronted with another dilemma. Should the fish be treated *in situ*, or be removed to a hospital tank? If they are treated in their aquarium there is the real risk that the medications may destroy the beneficial bacteria of the filter system, and this will increase your problems. Furthermore, many pathogens, once established in a closed body of water, may be capable of surviving the treatment in their spore stage. No sooner have you apparently overcome the

Aquarium hobbyists are able to take advantage of the many remedies and preventatives that have been formulated specifically for use with guppies and other tropical fishes. Photo courtesy of Aquarium Products.

problem than it reappears! The potential list of conditions and diseases in fishes is huge. With this fact in mind, this chapter is devoted mainly to prevention techniques and what to do in the event a problem is found. You should then refer to more detailed texts in order to try and pinpoint the cause of the problem.

Pet shops carry an extensive range of health products, and your dealer is the person to talk to if you suspect, or have, a problem. Most of the likely conditions you might encounter can be treated if these are dealt with promptly.

WATER CONDITIONS

Just about every disease and condition in aquaria are the result of a breakdown in care. Here is a list of *some* of the ways pathogens get into your aquarium and how to reduce the risk of their entering your water:

1) During the initial setting up of the aquarium you did not clean

every addition to it. Pathogens could thus have been present even before a fish was placed in the tank. Plants must be cleansed using an appropriate treatment from your pet shop. Rocks, gravel, and all decorations should be rinsed with very hot water before use.

2) The water should be "mature" and at the correct temperature before a single fish is added. If the nitrogen cycle has not been completed this will greatly stress the initial fish and raise the probability of a problem. Remember, a number of pathogens are ever present, no matter what you do. Do not stress the fish and give them an opportunity to attack!

3) The initial fish are best quarantined before being placed into a display tank. It is far easier to strip down a quarantine tank if problems are encountered than to do the same with a newly established system, complete with all of its decorations and extra water volume.

4) The initial and all additional fish should be obtained from a very reputable source, otherwise you will simply transfer their problems to your tanks.

5) Never risk overstocking the aquarium, as this can result in stressed fish. Such individuals are far more susceptible to illness than contented fish.

6) Ensure that routine cleaning is maintained on a regular basis and that all tools used are sterilized (hot water and/or a rinse in strong salt water) before and after each use.

THE QUARANTINE/HOSPITAL TANK

This is without doubt your best safeguard from transferring problems from the seller's tanks to your own, regardless of how good the seller's reputation is—even they can have problems. The tank can be small (5-10 gal) and should be sparsely decorated using artificial plants and small ceramic flowerpots to provide refuge. It will need a heater and a simple box filter, together with moderate to dim lighting. Make sure the water is the same temperature as that from which the fish are coming. During the quarantine period this can then be adjusted to that of your main aquarium if there is a difference.

The isolation period should be about 14-21 days. Add about one half a teaspoon of salt to each gallon of water, and this will prove beneficial in eradicating low levels of many bacteria. During the isolation period observe the fish carefully for signs of problems (to be discussed shortly).

In the event you are treating sick fish, add the medicine to the water as per the manufacturer's instructions only, assuming you have a positive diagnosis of the problem. Once the isolation/treatment period is over, adjust conditions back to those of your display tank and then reintroduce the fish to the main tank. Then strip the treatment tank and thoroughly clean it. Repeat this operation immediately before its next use.

IDENTIFYING PROBLEMS

There are two types of diseases in fishes. There are those that display some outward sign of their presence, and those that do not. Your attention will be focused on the former. If a number of fish start to die without displaying external signs, your first thoughts should be to the water quality and the possibility that there is a toxin. First, you should discuss the matter with a fish expert, preferably one who can examine the fish and your aquarium. A water specimen should be analyzed by a chemist if possible. At the very

pronounced, which may be too late. 1) Lack of appetite. In a large community of guppies it is easy to miss the fish that is not consuming its normal amount of food. 2) Erratic movements: This heading includes sudden darting across the tank for no reason, rubbing against hard objects, or swimming in a lopsided manner. The problem is probably parasitic or related to the swim bladder. 3) Breathing problems: The fish will gasp at the surface for air, and its gills will be

PHOTO COURTESY OF JUNGLE LABORATORIES.

Many different remedies, preventives and tonics are available at pet shops.

least, you should conduct the water tests (nitrite, pH, etc., discussed earlier) for a content list. Normally, however, fish will display some indication of problems and the following are some items to look for.

Behavioral oddities: Only by observing your fish on a daily basis will you become acquainted with each fish and its habits. Without this knowledge the chances are that you will only perceive a behavioral change when it is very

reddened and open. The problem may be parasitic, bacterial, or the result of excess ammonia or nitrites in the water, assuming aeration is adequate. 4) Listlessness: The fish seeks a refuge behind plants or decorations. It may rest on these, or the substrate, showing little interest in what else is happening in the tank. As it may be hidden from view, a head count of your fish will show up any that are missing.

Physical Signs: Any abnormal signs are unhealthy in your fish. These include swellings, abrasions, loss of color (dullness caused by excess mucus resulting from skin infection), missing bits of fins (these may result from nipping by other fish or from disease), spots, cotton-like growths, and visible parasites attached to the skin.

WHAT YOU SHOULD DO

The golden rule when applied to any potential illness is *Never do nothing.* If you decide to wait and see how things are tomorrow you may awake to see one or two fish, or an entire collection, floating on the surface or laying on the substrate, dead. You must note all of the physical and behavioral signs, as well as the water conditions (temperature, pH, nitrite, and so on). Relate these to your dealer and act on the advice given.

Clearly, you must decide on the severity of the problem. Is just one fish ill, or are many showing problems? If just one, then it should be removed immediately and placed in a hospital tank. If a number, much will depend on the illness or disease. Generally, if many fish are ill you might as well treat them in the main tank; raise the temperature a few degrees and effect the remedial treatment. However, if this route is taken it is suggested that once things are normal again the tank is stripped down and set up again. This is obviously time-consuming, but it may avoid a repeat of the problem. Transferring all of the fish to a hospital tank may not be practical (due to the size of tank needed) and could stress the fish, which is not recommended when they are already stressed by illness.

If fish are treated in the main tank, try to obtain medicines that will not kill the beneficial bacteria. Do not turn off the filter system at this time, because this will reverse the nitrogen cycle and prove counter-productive, though this could happen anyway if the medicines kill the beneficial bacteria. Even so, you still need the aeration and water circulation facility of your filter system. If the tank is heavily stocked it would be prudent to decrease the numbers as soon as possible in order to both reduce the risk of the spread of disease, and to reduce the pressure on the filter and aeration systems.

A Purple Glass Variegated Guppy produced by Gan Aquarium Fish Farm in Singapore.

Take out only those fish that seem very healthy. This action just might save a number of the fish from actually contracting what might prove to be a fatal disease that wipes out those that remain in the original tank.

GLOSSARY OF USEFUL TERMINOLOGY

Albino: A pure white animal that displays no pigment whatsoever. It is red-eyed. In guppies albinism is only partial, and restricted to the melanin pigments; thus, other colors such as yellows and reds can be seen.

Chromosome: The structure that carries genes.

Dominant: A gene that expresses itself visually when in single dose.

Epistatic: Said of a gene that is able to mask the presence of one or more other genes. Albinism is a typical example.

Filtration: A collective term applied to any process, be this mechanical, chemical, or biological, that removes unwanted substances (solids or gases) from a given volume of water.

Gamete: A male or female reproductive cell; a sperm or ovum (egg).

Gene: The basic unit of heredity.

Genotype: The total genetic composition of an individual, combining both visual and "masked" genes.

Hardness: An expression to indicate the amount of salts in a given volume of water. It can be measured in various ways, and may be temporary or permanent.

Heterozygous: An individual having unlike genes at a given locus, thus producing unlike gametes for the characteristic in question. Non-purebreeding.

Homozygous: An individual having like genes at a given locus, thus producing similar gametes for the characteristic in question.

PHOTO BY TANAKA.

Tanaka produced many mutants which were never sold internationally and thus have no name.

Purebreeding.

Locus (plural, Loci): The fixed position on a chromosome at which a gene, or one of its alternative forms (alleles), is located.

Mutation: A sudden change in the way a gene expresses itself. It creates an alternative characteristic (allelomorph) at the locus or loci of the gene(s) involved.

Oviparous: Egglaying. The embryos are nourished by the egg yolk and hatch outside of the female's body.

Ovoviviparous: Producing eggs that hatch in the oviduct of the female, but are not directly, or only partially, nourished by her. Livebearing.

Ovum: An egg; the sex cell of the female.

pH: A logarithmic scale that is used to indicate the acidity or alkalinity of water based on the number of hydrogen and hydroxide ions present. pH 1.0-6.9 is acidic, pH 7.0 is neutral, and pH 7.1-14.0 is alkaline.

Phenotype: The visual appearance of an individual. Two fish may have the same phenotype, but may not breed alike. Their

recessive's presence.

Sex-linkage: The state that exists when the heredity of a gene is located on a sex chromosome is linked to the sex that carries it. Genes located on the X chromosome can be passed to either sex, those on the Y chromosome can be inherited only by the males.

Species: A group of animals that will interbreed in the wild and are reproductively isolated from all

A champion double swordtail guppy developed and photographed by Tanaka

visual similarity may derive from different genotypes.

Poecilia reticulata: The current scientific name for the guppy.

Polygenic: Said of a characteristic that is inherited on a quantitative basis involving many genes, for example, size.

Recessive: A gene that must be present on both chromosomes of a pair in order to be visually apparent. The exception is a gene carried on the sex chromosome—a sex-linked gene, where no locus exists on the other sex chromosome of a pair, so there can be no dominant gene to mask the

other groups. The lowest obligatory rank in a formal classification.

Sperm: The sex cell of the male.

Viviparous: Producing eggs that are retained within the uterus of the female where they are nourished by her. Livebearing.

Wild type or Normal: Terms used in genetics to indicate the natural phenotype of a species as compared with any mutational forms.

Zygote: An ovum that has been penetrated by a sperm, resulting in a fertilized egg that contains all of the genetic material for the new individual.

INDEX